I0759571

PACES THE CAGE

S*an D. Henry-Smith

The Song Cave

For the band(s) I m in—what mosses!, twill, yet unnamed,
perhaps to remain nameless, Black Boots, Depth Address, mouthfeel,
Fernet Negro, Dark Around the Edges, sunchoke, PhantomSun,
other arrangements still taking shape.
I hope to always show up to you sharp.

To Perla, sweet fleeting trill—

The Song Cave
www.the-song-cave.com

Cover Image © Janiva Ellis, *Listen to the Soul Warrior*, 2023. Courtesy of the artist and 47 Canal, New York
Design and layout by Janet Evans-Scanlon

ISBN: 979-8-9912988-6-5
Library of Congress Cataloguing-in-Publication Data has been applied for.

FIRST PRINTING

CONTENTS

Landscape sets the rhythm for this improvisation.
There are many ways this could go.
May our love be resplendent—
We had to make it up as we went along.

I've lost interest in potential & grown attached
to what is happening, the present happening,
& its backmatter
—Imani Elizabeth Jackson, *Context for Arboreal Exchanges*

Perhaps, then, the moment has
come to talk In lieu of offering documentary proof
—Akilah Oliver, *a(August)*

I demand the right to assess the worth of my own life.
Who else could open such an involute dark
—Anthony McNeill, *Chinese Lanterns from the Blue Child*

in & for voices

my my my
my my my my m y
mmn my my my
Mmm my my
mmmmhm
my my my my my my myhymy mym y
m ym mymy myyy mhy muy my my m y muh my my

my my
my

my my my m ymyaah my m y
hmy mm my muh hmmu
my m my my my my my my ma my ma my my ma mu my hmma my my
mu my mi my my MY my my hmma hmmuha mmyy mymy my my my
my
my
my mhuy my my my
my mmhu ma my
ym mh my my m
hma mhy my
my my

my

my

my mu mu mhu ma muh my my my
my mh mh mh
mmy mmy mmu myhu my   my my

mmmhm

mazed in the skull / in search of simpler language / tied & versioning knot /
whisper / watermouth / the shape of roaming / deliberate /

/

/

/

mouth settles into itself / differently / gums / slime about teeth /
weathered relative to use /

/

/

/

/

/

hot gas that is Will passes between them / follicles of enamel forming beak /
dull bird that I am: speak /

dull bird that I am: speak

/

that I am: speak /
timbre that I am: burns /

they will do to you what they did to the others / should you wait your turn.

sense unnamed / remain to us
secrecy
/ let s go down where you are / let s go down
where
yes , let s go down /
let s go down where
you are /

in search of simpler language, tell me what is available,
simply / greedy, one fool
absorbs to diminish
all do then clutch shadow s crouch /
in depth particulate /
premature midnight recalls cloven four, tail, & twin-throat horned prince/

what fool feels for history : what|which|ever narrative
makes just|absolves his system of value /
feigned to cycles, in which turns
everything at fringe ,
innumerable

they will do to you what they did to the others / should you wait your turn.

longing babble moans geyser diaphragmic
wombs unique pressure of speech
umbilical deft spills

in the suspended state of murmur
all things live

murmur   little murmur
little murmur little
murmur
building a little place in a little murmur

thunder   little thunder
little thunder little
thunder
building a little storm in a little murmur

flint to spark. much lift! must fall! much lift! must fall! much lift! must fall! grinding stompweight. heel-tossed soil meshes malevolenttrance. there is no stage. only the round. there is only this threshold, this floor we hold. yea, here memory conjures. open palm to howling skin. what mattered most was that it happened at once. in search of an expanding language, I could only bleed. in search of simpler language, I could only ***HA***.

HA. simple as it was. simple as it were. simple as it may be. a language enveloped another & left out our family name. twin-throated

bubble forth in
murmur
unclenched to roar *much lift!*
must fall!

full clip for the head of state why wait

self-noise

make amble cut—wed by miraculous, press to make true. grove to mark
time like groove. groove to make time w/ you. it dawns on us: facing down.
O—to be in that music   & to be in that sound, the lengths I d go!
the lengths I d go—

o

errant heretic, stand in the mirror:
an image takes hold of you now. boy: from cockscomb grows fawn-necked
& alert, head a-tilt, face greased like Sunday. bow at the part of his lip now
pulled to war. trilling true voice trined dissonant, he proposes a strategy:

○

There would be a Great Rupture,
After which All will Change.
How you know me Now will be
Different from how you knew me
Then. The remaining Promise is
Time, that Total Entity w/ which we
Are obliged to negotiate.

○

continuing, voice split crisp to rasp—
forego the need for Silence, let what
Was. a/tonal Pleasure in ongoing expression surrounds us like a Moss,
bark before log, seed before trunk, forest Before Bloom. held below,
branching up. flesh-ripe for experiment, castor-rich. a root retains
its Bitter—

○

we tear from the same eye
Teacher: I am your pupil

°

—the initiate demands the sound—volume, her ministry—technique to mask blend—she furls the sorting hole—let it be—god of tremor so what—sleep evades us—in saline resemblance she prays—brine of the sweated glass you hold hot encumbered nowhere ear of a dying god now dead—kindly, kindling—rabbit s foot holds her sounding hand—knob management—pace of hop—not that obvious death, but that it is meaning gut—she insists on live—it could not be expected—long voluminous—beautiful revenge—she doesn t lose keys—vibrato—in lyric silence await a world for the word—gut the sound—throw it back—flash,—she chose it—cut it off—fuck it—ballistic—telescopic—long-range—she lives—prayerfully—unbound—Mother loves the girls she s made—she is one of them—she makes herself—one—

○

in the wind
weepfully free
—release it!
drooling sob,
set me free—

o

(i) allow me my incomplete› my half-step body ears wet w/ listening› five after fire we said we need a new wild› an exodus from the fatal haunt of expectation› renewed beyond a well that can be sold› bottled wellness› the ceasefire will not suffice› we need a new wild› bulling waltz› feral haircut for a hill› bolted knuckle› pale stain of rain› blissfully occupying criminal position

○

the elegiac moan is operative› I would live for you› hermetic no longer› she loans him her conduit diaphragm› circular breathing rounds complete› uncompressed› at capacity› desperate to make round› voice w/o flourish treads hush››

airbodybreathvoice | , self-noise | immolate hiss

›› heat of

presence overwhelms› hearing wire holds its sound› attuned to hearing› hiss of thought | hiss of ambient› current of nothing› dead currency stay dead› no objective anything› dust to needle grits warmth› scrapes against presence› the record infiltrates› anyway you spin it

○

another disappeared poet—among whom I tulle—
warriors of smeared word smeared by word—the first to be sacrificed—
to silence the griot is the culture of the cull—to sever memory—*but the*
body—maestro animates the corpse—let us live for you

—hell-bent in immediate—wonderfully imperfect
—in the face of the flame—trust empassioned—true trine true
—the unfathomable rapts me up—succumb to it—*take hold of me*—

○

the woman I love tosses a pot of water to stone—splash! strikes blade to it like match let it spark! withdrawal let it burr! she says *take me home, or take me underground, we ain t got time to waste. you wanna watch, or you wanna do something?* the best we can keeps getting a little worse. maybe was a place we could hope to be. hotter & still hotter days.

○

intercessor s droning monologue beads a sweat about her brow. pitched to a falling bell. lung, a window, be. she stands gap between Worlds—that alone zeroth the imposed shudder of shame. the jolt of transition greater than that of all fear the tease of liberation s haunt

○

air greed | excess | w/o identifiable purpose or function | insistent | that which functions beyond evidence | that which produced a/rhythmic order | try this gait for size | let this life be the site of ongoing experiment | my own life mine lawless | for now | this, my body

made strong toward impulse.

○

O—the noise that makes my body mine
& the noise that makes me—
let me hear it clearly
          hear it more

remedies I

what can I know of this life but what it cost me? pretending to
love these patterns of negotiation, pretending the Doubleworld
was acceptable—the Skin beneath the Skin made hell of our hell,
the Source from which the Source draws rectifies its embellishment,
reifies its abandon. Another way: in a room filled w/ overturned
bottles, the ceiling fan turns, knowing not the relief it provides,
but damns w/ its clicking; we lie awake at night wondering would
it be better to sweat out our sheets, turn the thing off. we remember
stillness as we enact it, hoping to quiet our body as to cool it.

&

briefly

I recall how slowly Granny eat,

I see her in her dining room chair.

us girls amidst girls wield the weaving material scattered kaleidoscopic. Recognition beyond sight, the apparatus of vision pressed against glass. Gender discontinuum, flesh of collected invention obliged to my own social contract.

Tooth against tooth, braced into breaking. One dream I do not write down, its viscera remains. It arrives again no less familiar; toolless defanging, making room in the mouth for gumming. Twin mirror averse syncing into study spins of Juturna. The bloodied canines in my palm do not render me powerless—now there s a new way to whistle.

lip /

laps dew at the margin of mouth. alchemic spittle
at the behest of cusses foul. tongue chewed short in
concentration. from the top! & this time, w/ teeth—

mid/riff

for sol cabrini

belldrivers plugged to tremor garnishing a muscular lick in bellybutton-out weather. when locked into notary maze, vagrant, channel an absent fuzz, my dear.

skirt&flare in dual follow; let me show you how to dial a pulse,
            hear the song s teach

humblescribe lapse tentacle drag to crawl. sunkissed scrapes at an inhospitable skin wound eerie. scratch a granular catalyst. pulling nimble follow gazing out an auspicious thing needling lace.

she likes it telesonic | I m a bitch that plays the bridge pudgy in the middle, grit barks when I dig.

harping willows—you & I—*harping meadows* surrendering present. & my
sibling 'round the way a rowdy listener—that s RaFia—groove
optometrist. my witness. monic clash knead tough the speaking muscle
to a beating tremolo, thumbing humble to heart. *if i pause, it s only because*
I m in awe

course return albeit tilt: why wave out so far? *just wanted to see.*
music for driving at dawn, adrift tenses low, lazy. there s enough for us here.

throw from the shoulder / creeping dagger s rain—
            peel at a tear, pick at a scab

devoice

you long like them to be porous
winded in the breathless city, its filthy menagerie. dressed like a sail—
twirling in the handsome rain

your abundant novice blows the horn
Loverboy, will you die on the moon?
How does it go again, my Carolina?
my flower
my grain & my flower

ghetto sonetto foul play (exist strategy)

grave

we should end w/ a question was what this melody takes
on, the whole way through. Bird dug deeper into a coup.

by time I knew it was noise, I was knee deep. this flare—
it comes from the chest. bebop is in the pocket,

dare the arising string-up. shovel dig in the lip. sectional behavior
stations same, pierce of the spade. yellow metal makes rust of his hands.
choke,

what you on about. it was taken / it was let go. for your tarnish,
I whisper death. a required problem. the approach foretold—

spit in the palm. technology the shape of its
media. drain its flow. want it over w/ so bad, might just do
a good job.

led the horse to an empty well. & the train I missed always came too early.
train
I m on always drags so slow. wow you move made genre—

birds of paradise squawk an ailment, a festering sound
surprise me w/ something other than cruelty.

got had at

the changes!

the sound of now? *noise.* I don t know what to tell you—
maybe it was love,
maybe r&b, metronome drones *grave*

remedies II

at the point in which I had finally found the courage to sleep
(3 on either side of the clock, beauty waits for no one & my
intention is to catch up w/ it) the absolute worst thing to fixate
on as extended metaphor regarding displacement & morality,
steps onto center stage, shadow visible before figure:
the grooming practices of daddy longlegs, foot in mouth,
one
          at   a   time
drives me into my twisted burrowing net. you can have
the whole bed! sheets too, honey. daddydaddy longlegs crawlin'
cross my bed again, 33 minutes after 3 on either side of the clock,
on either side of the clock.

sundew

intertidal meshes sublunary you
plunged in tall grasses
organ, giggle stick
whimpering hold—problems worth having
cyprine, your morning smirk
plunged in tall grasses

it was a flood

you wear me closely
time s doving call

you wear me over
like a skin

full air exceeding
the (toll
      tool
      woe
      call) of voice

dull drills a fluent
marbling

whenever pouring
it s now & then

it s all surrounding
like a wind
/
it s now/never
all the time

some time we re spending
time spent I m bought

it s now or never
all the time
/
it s all surrounding
like a thought

The greenhouse became its own time signature.

for Derica, Rehema, Sumu, & Zahra, who held voice in the house, & AZ OOR, w/ whom I huddled

Outside, there were other voices. They
listened w/ kept distance. The house
kept close its conversation. Small gusts

moved what was fur. There were 100
windows around us, then—maintaining
a faint perimeter. Latent radio, your

laughter came in waves. Again in the
Outside—the Walled City held its
riches: the river-envy of neighbors.

The tributary proximity catalyzes a
frustration about false caves, &
icicles for waking bats, for which

Bunny shoots the footage. The Garden
spoke of what they spoke of. Curious,
we inched toward the tweeter,

as if to catch up. Badmind was the
Panopticon, Evil Eye. Day made
still its declines. All things wet made

its drip.

mbira quintet

err of unnatural proportions, it takes the might of two to play each.
tooth of the machine makes sound-language loose.
tribal strategy to spirit, tribute to welcome spirit—
exoskeletal hand treasures the click of tin, tranducent Mukwa,
calling you here to us.
carrying box bellows calabash—
—announcing torrent trill—deadlessresounding—

IN COMMON KIND crouched in crowd, triangulated in listening
thinker emphatic holds court on the talking bench
sorrow s daughter finds laughter, sorrow s daughter finds laughter
time s tender takes no toll, webbing dusk s compromise. o' my
sisters take sisterhood serious as a shadow, what feints in her light
pales separate to possessive, stoop-sat **BODYFAST**
trove of a lover s ear, quietly curled rigid. ridged. sunflower censored—
—troughs yearning rolls in June s delight
returning to this world thrice-winged, patient.

carnival

I see my son in a thousand eyes
are you free to be angry?
surrender

to a well another, , , ,

there! the smoking mound jumps to memory, before I ve reached the door. or light so lambent, it fogs. phone in the mirror. all journeys accumulate here:

home,

heart,

head. matters of observation, chance patterns, realm of spirit. solo voyager, will you meet me? in the world? I cannot make sense of it alone—

ghost road of raring ability, what a day. slope, stream, sudden glowing field. all so sudden?

through the house of sudden windows, to a well
another,
,
,
,
,
,
,

twoing axes split the trunk,
& memory scores a play.
(what s the point?)

twoing shadows arch out
into senescent deep,
well overflowing another.

twoing scale spells a funny
puzzle, becomes an untruing
triptych, doorless edifice.

another,
,
,
,
,
,
,

collector of wishes spent the currency of dreams. the way I walk, I wear through the sole: at the edge & on my toes, the fool. will what broke gravity remain unchanged?

there was a faint trace of encounter—
an encumbering, total abeyance.

what fell those trees, too fell me,
feet splayed asunder, so.

borrowed image

Talk the stories of night. That fella there was a dense kiss. Associate of liminals, name another such intimacy. Galaxy, I showed you my bad side. So then, was it not worth throatedness? Grant me ruthless access to the psychological image, discomfortable mercy. Granted, *he loved him madly—*

All hands fell fair in the fight, as to offer lament—we would not come clean from this. None of us. Slip trace. Peacemaker, Ankh-ringed, looking down a bridge. Smug about her room tone: *It is not fair to place on you the problem of audience, it is simply not fair. & so what of it? A curator is but a series of poses.*

I will miss what we once were in the aftermath, handsome viper in my garden. He dares me to forget. We deal in the unseen business, puppets making puppets of a/ether. Standing here, I have to ask you, on the off-chance no one else has: you felt the need to carry here this dirt? Pound for pound, no?

Time s hole, no? Ardid spore. There could be no victor. There could be no forget, taking envy in the terrible beauty distributed. *I ll be around.* They picture your hunting eyes—your face of framing. Slip trace. Expression s farce dance. We did not concern each other. Hardly worth the call, wired to the

wall. In the evasive square, I had hoped we might see past our differences. What can I say? I m nostalgic for Pan-Africanism & the ozone layer. Reparations: The Game Show. Gold to bone as you go higher. *I ll be around.* Farce slip. Freedom runs its unfinished course. Unsigned elisions, contractions. Catastrophic how meek I am just waiting. Being who work makes us! The distance is unbearable, & so the proximate. Breath automatic singed in a tight grin. Can t fast track the lived. Humidity seeks a window through which to flee. Steam paints a mirror of drip.

w/ no fore-warning, a dog guards what was once my hallway. He belongs to no one, himself; this is now where he lives; he stands it w/ his life; snug where I bury my bone.

((((((((STOP))))))))

after Bill Gunn s *Stop*, 1970

cursed by involvement, but she would not suffer the same death. the wife of the poet halts recess into echo over snowbanked decadence; tower is the lover s freefall, screech of a landing plane. never pleasure s immeasurable window the aerial reshapes the room, glamour trails their trouble. people who are used to being served lose themselves w/o service. unveiled: statuettes marking absented line the blemished mansion. level madness—unleash haunt for master. smartly tailored, day has not changed. sex of arrival laying claim like a pissing dog. possessive acts. Michael parts an obstacle to Lee, her obstacle. cut to their laughter. *come on* he says–as if to say that would be too easily resolved. lizard stands wait on the arm of the chair. they laugh & laugh. the spell unfolds. aerial divulges the god-eye of true psychedelia.

how did it happen? the frightening reality bursts into an upheaval, thriller s structure: man s resentment for the failure of the individual & being responsible for someone beside himself—exaggerated by debauchery s long sleep & his embarrassing unwillingness to be vulnerable|penetrable, unable to hold *her fluttering presence w/in myself,* & needing someone to blame for that—seeks to displace himself in suicidal impulse morphing into brutal hunt for the vessel of sensitivity or paranormal empathy he lacks & envies. mad, he hunts her.

not again, her halting palm pulls the strings. two in jewels & white dresses, salute to she who insists on her labor s earning; she will not be a pawn—business is business. *nothing should be illegal.* & she who insists on her keep becomes unabashed at his lessoning respect, playing her accused female game. suffer no quiet about her wisdom. strength of gentle when betrayed.

half-full smile voices reversal s rushed violins. sustained exhibitionist, watching the pecking cock learned to be these men shouting for fight until they tire. practice his arena for letting into, service frame. butler & slave, who is to be paid? the sex of the dinner party jesters intellect s game at the threat of sex. wide-eyed at the lip of glass, a true prop touches lip thumbing cool to her forehead. suggestive eats carnations, the sex of summer below the clavicle. fade way to her world, a dizzying stare. the Caribbean whistles in—drop by drop by drop. waterslick panning a panting sky, 2/3s in a splice. blade between the legs. *you re beautiful* charms a swinger, coming home to your chaos. Angel s proxying assault on the sprawl of good carpet, raising your head to the froth. *I m stronger than you, Michael.* Gunned, their haunt. red might be your color. to mark you dead & mine. tongue to the devil s cleft,

(((((((((*you get caught up*)))))))))

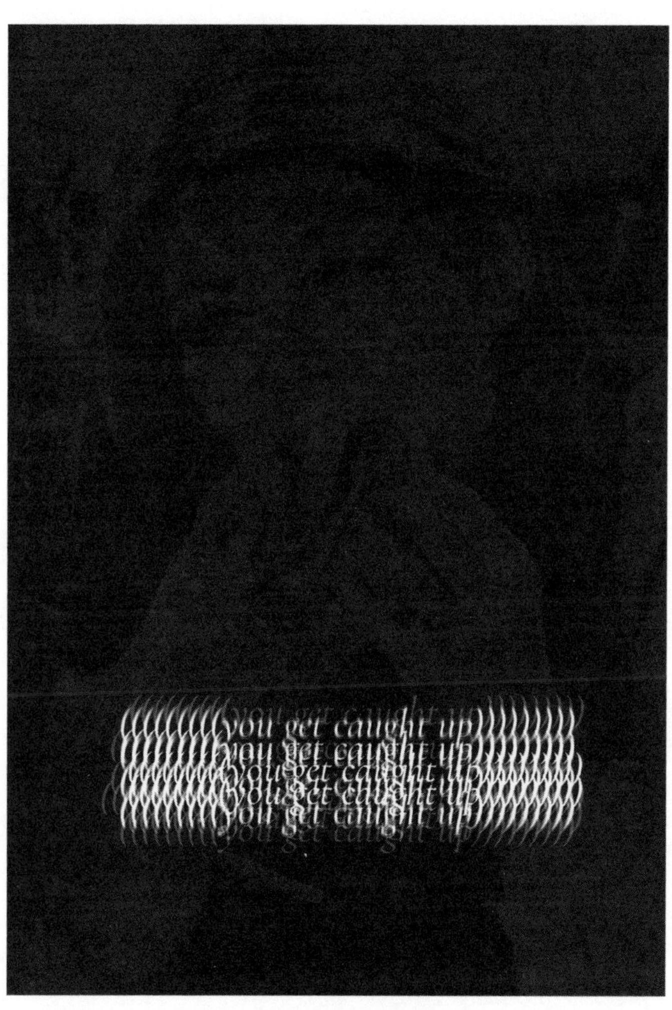
you get caught up
you get caught up
you get caught up
you get caught up
you get caught up

remedies V

/ heavy altar (no elevation),

miracle trodden, thumb turning bead. The Crystal Diggers knew it true: reorient devotion to ground–uncontained, in its own order. walls slipping holy, singing dually lean on into fervor.

praise at the collapse. Breath of Burning, weightless silver saunters in gravitational cycloning downward, toward that which is absorbent. & for this, *what can you withstand? what will you let go?*

s t o n e b o o m

after Beverly Buchanan s *Untitled (Frustula Series)*, 1978

1.

dolostone blast unearths an earth. HiFi of her hand. h o l e tone. stacked horizon—heard weight. *heavy.* imagined aggregate moored by ante-intrathermics. yes, a heat that stills. hydrates a compound listening structure, honoring the amalgamous sound. mound altar keels over tall. mark my word.

2.

hark—this tune. heeds predicate suggestion.
monitor the treble congregate pleasant surrender — press
to know the soft release of glass &
magnet, oh, you curious child. sliders, knobs,
buttons: let it rearrange you.
daddy said don't touch. listen up. blissed
out in sustenant ruins. rehearsing numbers in
segmented display: resets at InfinityFM. stone altar solid rock
solid. let it slide, let it boom —
l e t i t s l i d e , l e t i t b o o m

3.

humors of a stone rope—
— pile high as you like. harper of a stone harpgrumble
truth the string (how it heaves!
            ,*heavy*). fiddling at the floor of her stereo,
            liquidus, tensile proclamation!   so long—the habit
            of separating things, bleed beyond   cell, isolate no longer.
linger past   slimestone of a
musique concrète.   unshapes   consummate sound— let slurry become stone.
          idle pleasure. ruinous altar,
                                        my plaything puddles   h i g h
                                                                    h i g h
                                                                          h i g h
                                                                    h i g h

may it remain unchartered, chatter of latesinging
mockingbirds, it is daybreak no matter when
awakened. how else to halt the haunting but to
avoid the night? all but half the haul, 9^2, hoarse
w/ remembering. **a/mercurial** inevitabilities bend
what was anticipated, flout an already broken
relativity. you speak tenderly amidst the swelling
air, spoke of leap years somberly, I dare not
repeat the spell.

exponential, the volume of rose bush where you
live, blushed forth in bloom second & third &
fourth. useless in your eagerness to
learn all things in part, to part as you please.
burning all over, bruised fruit, baby what a bramble
we tussle. worn thin by the ambition, darting
through thorn throne, twig metropolis. you take it
all for granted. returning to nest empty,
mocking its nature.

Never created, never destroyed, eternal wave of light adhered to present reality. The precise sampling of air w/in air, pressed, stretched, & folded, the edges aligned in perfect touch. Synchronous accumulation propels toward this very grand particular, particulate augmentation orients ordering toward negotiating transference, magnitude beyond measure, at every turn an experiment in extending the same great breath, making it whole, being wholly enveloped by it. Native intangibilities solidified & expressed as language under imposed language, Kamau Brathwaite reminds us we already knew how to talk, & here again the sunhot dust of the Earth kicked up instinctive rhythmic response, cloud of propelled candor backchat held back long as we needed to. A divergent state ushers us along. Stuttered & chanted vocal fluctuation burped & bounced, crystalline ignition, an attempt at the world: there is how we speak, then there is what we say.

Such is the act of the frame, precise suctioning w/in the vacuumous multitude. Or one way to turn on it, or the angle from which I m witnessing: Robert Moog offers Quincy Jones a new tool & he hears the horn a new way, & America hears a synth on TV for the first time, *Iron Side* a bleeding siren the year before the year we re heading back to. 36 years later there it is in *Kill Bill*, the blaring horn born synth reminds of vicious memory. Never created, never destroyed—one of her last samples. All the new sound is organic. The ground proves itself ready to become tomorrow every day, ready to facilitate another form, *Black Origami* folding back into yesterday, what was this paper before it was this shape? Jlin in Gary, Indiana knows the machine by hand, built it in an Automobile City. Yesterday, it was *Nationtime—Gary* right very there & William Greaves was thinking about the First Law of Thermodynamics when he was making *Symbiopsychotaxiplasm* in 1968. In 1972 he s still thinking about group dynamics, & how important it is when Black people get together, even if we don t know what we want, even if we don t want the same thing. Maybe it was just to get together. Maybe it was 1972. We are mourning men, following the widows who held them up, who in turn are asked to uplift other men.

On his own dime, Greaves films the National Black Political Convention; four slides in & he has brought us to the Atlantic—reminding us Middle Passage brings us only this far. See, Arkestra implies the boat, the many. Because this far leaves us still in struggle. The Chairman of the Congress of Afrikan People, Imamu Amiri Baraka is speaking to the delegations, he offers himself as their servant. In the music, *Nationtime* talking w/ African Visionary Music, Motown/Black Forum in the Black forum, still 1972. *Can you imagine something other than what you see?* He s asking. I wanna know why Michigan really walked out. I want to know what happened to that heartbeat, where I failed it.

On stage, Sister Betty Shabazz is talking to Mrs. Corretta Scott King, voice to ear. The breath supported hush intended for one other in the clamor of the high school gym, conference going, heated. Sister Shabazz is looking straight on Mrs. King s profile, eyes searching.

We spend some decades in a wandering lost, perfecting exclusions en caste. Just as bad, twice as fast. An isolating climate fell over. Preoccupied w/ how to survive this shore, *counting T-cells*. Another conference preoccupies my reflection, Black Nations/Queer Nations? & its film of the same name, 1995, directed by Shari Frilot. A 3-day gathering held three years after Audre Lorde s passing on, held by her instruction: *The fact that we are here and that I speak these words is an attempt to break that silence and bridge some of those differences between us, for it is not difference which immobilizes us, but silence. And there are so many silences to be broken.* 1995: SILENCE=DEATH, the commitment to volume.: M. Jacqui Alexander, Cheryl Clarke, Cathy Cohen, Kendall Thomas, & our director organize 600 lesbians, gay men, bisexuals, & transgendered people of African descent thinking critically toward our survival, choosing queer as our unifying term, as a working class term. Struggling over this long shore. Dedicated to Essex Hempill, among his last moments w/ us on record—his voice shapes our concern.

As our enemies unite across borders, so must we—border a disorientation. We unify a sample made & in-making, grounding secularity s necessary betrayal & subtle propensity for Pentecostal decorum. The sample irons fragment, memory s hold. Just sum to feed on flowering new field. *I ll take you there*, The Staples Singers anthemic plays out throughout, sampled & cut to punctuate overlapping speech, reading, panel, & working group revelation. *BN/QN* artifacts a queer '90s & the aesthetic decisions that entails: direct-to-camera address, performative & poetic delivery, patterned & nonlinear transitions, camp s chilling comedy, read the room. Sampling a source that teaches—Marlon Riggs' oeuvre, his obvious influence sings. Just past three decades gone by, until when again—ideally outside of the market s parade. I attach to Samuel Delaney s defining & offering: yes, much beleaguered. If by term, community is more accurately sized, nation is destination & metaphor—faith & conjure, speculative weapon against vulnerability, w/out the bleed of gun-lust nation wields shameless.

Still, nation paces the hall of my mind like a disease. World-infringing world, witness & refuse the total whole of disposability. Broad stroking gore, riot out of grave. Industrial—the sound, the condition. Tony Cokes, *Black Celebration* (1988), his talking screen flashing lyricism s direct address in clashing materialities, a collaborative text. Los Angeles burns in repetition, yesterday in commodity s black & white rainbow, the riot where you seek relinquish, economy of theft & gift, just sums for the oppressed. Nation notions mass, ooze commodity. Depreciation, swelling pledge & primrose. Everything that fails to flourish, its notion means what on stolen land. We inhabit a burial ground. Land art its mimicry ergo, denied grave. Beverly Buchanan s slow eroding memorial arranges an engagement w/ Earth over nation, hidden in present excess, use-value s disregard. The inherent value of our life & burial, turn stone, turn. Pebbling speak. Nation you fetish collapse, kill family for sustenance. Those were the conditions: every kingdom sent their worst in the mask of a slain god. Their crimes, gently named, enforce our participation. Conspiratory soil grumbles strategy: *A Heavy Nonpresence* (2021)—Derica Shields, loyal to voice, convenes a private collective of communal strategists in oral history, bearing nation s insult, besting its game, & dispersing their tactics. Shields by name, carefully anonymizes their effort, honoring the haptics & dangers of strategy. We are our welfare, nation farewell. All in for all is the only way out.

Speculative: the colonizing entity dispatches a reconnaissance. Spy, you spy. The agents defy the mission. *The Changing Same* (2001), Cauleen Smith as director, writer, producer, & alien—star-descended star, prepares a future document. Before we make face of voice, he calls report, naming his sickening isolation for which he pleads home—his nation, double-bind: *they don t call me anything | I don t call them anything.* Thundering & digital screech, hazed & delayed in lightyear. He is denied in service of his deteriorating state, his punishment for obedience. His ambush makes action of desperation, unjustly enacting his rage onto an ally—as many such men. Her warrant distrust speaks naivety to their subjagation—not yet privy to nation, her duty & barrier. Leaps a stone bridge onto cracked tar. Centuries of altered histories, favoring one, lest we forget. They encourage our belief in the cell. Meer incubators nowhere seen. *You didn t recognize me?* Brave so to be for each other, at clarity s risk & treasure. Delicate witness, torrential. 'Cause what s the point when nothing feels good, hasn t since time. *What I choose to release | What I sacrifice to be complete.* Fragment is the form she chooses, exile unassigned, a new mission exhaled. Denied, she chooses her suffocation. *I am benign / if I am profane & incomplete / nothing will change.* Send signal, send word. Look for my love in the rebellion we inherit & to come, plan to be there for the first day.

—

David Greaves—the budget & production manager, assistant editor, second camera operator for *Nationtime—Gary*, & William s son—tales of filming together w/ his father, watching intimately the ecstatics of coalition, the crowd & the stage. In a surge, they seek the scene, & he, unexpectedly out of film, turns to find his father zealously working through zoom, whole body in the swing of seeing. Back in the editing room, the film is nowhere to be found. William, smiling wistful: *There was no film in the camera. It was such a great shot; I didn t want to miss it.*

PRACTICE *ETERNAL*

one fell swoop
one foul sweep
two then follow
down the hhole
two then follow
down the hhole
two then follow
down the hhole
two then follow
down the hhole
two then follow
down the hhole
two then follow
down the hhole
two then follow
down the hhole

one fell swoop
one foul sweep
two then follow
down the hhole

gross fero -cious
sim -mer down

groundseek
wake wake wake
walk walk walk

sleep
night by quickly

groundsee
wake wake wake
walk walk walk

dirt grit
gro wl
re/turn me, mythical
ear th *I wa-lk*

I wa-lk

I wa-lk
I wa-lk
inthe half-felled rain

a/ether

(time, what then turns flesh to

leather

earth

ear

surely surely surely surely surely surely surely
surely surely surely surely surely surely surely
there you are in the library of errors, where many our day s spent

what water runs | runs free
rushing to meet water
what water water s water
wavering over
water

waters into water
what pours into you pours me
-mory what water runs | runs free
rushing to meet memory

I wa-lk
inthe half-felled rain
I wa-lk
through the fog I—

where-I-go-where-is-it-where-I-go-where-is-it-where-I-go-where-is

DUB STRUCTURE
DUB STRUCTURE
DUB STRUCTUREDUB STRUCTURE
DUB STRUCTURE
DUB STRATA
DUB STRUCTURE
DUB STRUCTUREDUB STRUCTURE
DUB STRUCTURE
DUB STRUCTURE
DUB STRUCTURE

drunk mosquito
mind your business   *I m in the middle of something*
mind your business

all my toys are a little broken
& that s what makes them my toys

all my toys are a little broken
& that s what makes them my toys

let ‘em play | *let ‘em play* | *let ‘emPLAY*

there are drums in the distance
the World we are calls me forward

a was h   of rhyth ms   between t his p ulse
the void of home blooms. This place: I could not fill it, but
I   could attempt to hold it

rea(l)m
 rea(l)m
real
 real so it seems
rea m so it seems
 rea m so it seems
 so it seems
so it seams
 so it seams

voice versa
devoid of vice
voice- the
device of verse

exit strat -egy:
borrow|ed atrocity
fatigu- ing
su-bject s interlaced assonance& the
principle challenge of belief

a currency of
curiosity /owes
fear no debt

this is how we m a k e our ee t e r n a l

I relate to the tape in an abstract way. in this room I became incomplete. souls speak a shivering skip. an honest fixation building the immediacy of recall & response, on which we build further. *make your transition*. now, your turn: gripping on its angles. if you could drink me, then so down let me go. we are thread together in the map. press to square. grizzly pearls leak rotten, tracing urinary ideas. the circular bears the membrane. promiseless, hyperdocumented. just here what we have—beg we make it here now. tape, a shaky string, reels gratuitous. 37 seconds more. breath sustained the possibility of reaching something outside notation.

fluting barge —
                    w i l d
let it run—keep the w in d in
                    w i l d

[come around come around
/come around
this is how we PRACTICE*e t e r n a l*

come around come around
come around
thisishow*we*   p r a c t i c e   e t e r n a l

come around
come around
come around
this is how we mourn our   e t e r n a l come around

come around   come around
this is how we   m a k e   our ee t e r n a l
p r a c t i c e
p r \a c t i ce
p r a c t i c ee t e r n a l e t e r n a l pr a c ti c e et e r na l   p r a c t i c e e t
e r n a l p r a c t i c e   e t e r n a l]

X s out

tell down hard
on steady in/cline.

tell me

how

you ll
never be a fast -talker

two then follow
down the hhole

pull a rabbit
from the river

fissure / measure *for s.b.*

make no   illicit address
          roam at the ilk of his wander
          rule of thumb pinches salt of the slug

hair of the   chest   panel overlay makes apparent the corner we may
otherwise
ignore   /perhaps the practice of sculpture is to make evident the room
          —shoddy/ one may call his means

unaddressed
  addressed to inter   /lining
chop it up any way   that way—the unit is established, performing
predetermined,

rather than empirical (played w/ Duchampian charm—)
concentric navigation of an imperfect box creaks its floor

fissure / measure
            fissure/measure
fissure / measure
fissure / measure
            fissure/measure
fissure / measure

Event of the meter marks machine economy /eugenic upswing &
The Division of Africa,—right down the middle,
split made to seam

/all the way to newly united Paris, Berlin conferences convivial, False
Madrid, Brussels, Aarhus, Accra, Kinshasa, Eindhoven to Kralendijk to
Kyoto, Jakarta, & the Paramibo Express. Porto Novo, Dordrecht, SA.
São Paulo, Praia, Perrine, Montreal unreal, both Saint Martins, both
Bluefields, Jewsland, Chrtisiana, London dutty, making ash of its citizens.

ell any way we are set to go—

—pins in a self-justifying map   blank to the ugly of Europa

the World

carved by spoon   knife   &ruler

passed overhand—
even money was not enough   simple-mass needed expendable
&   the herd exhibited strange behavior
fissure / measure
fissure/measure
fissure / measure
fissure / measure
fissure/measure
fissure / measure

units   a   line   makes

steel gut filled of physical text   dissolutes standard

auda   -city of empty

audible

marks a man who chooses his visible step

gait material   measuring on unstandard

fissure / measure
fissure/measure
fissure / *measure*

Burn Mayflowers,

Burn
Mayflowers, sludge in the late night
sleep w/ the light on
eyes open, full of rage
seamstress, wrapped in sacred denims

worn thin in the pit
worn thin in the pit

w/
where w/ all, everyone together now
steal back the precipice
everyone, together now
wicked, racing hungry demons

worn thin in the pit
worn thin in the pit

twelve
times over, atemporal ritual
sleep w/ the light on
eyes open, full of rage
trouble, feeding empty bellies

worn thin in the pit

ONE NIGHT ONLY

featuring Mosie Romney s *One Woman Show,* 2023

(STAGED FOR THE ROUND)

SPOTLIGHT
YEAH, THAT S MY CUE
NOT HAVING IT—

THORAX WOVEN IN PRESENCE TENSE
FULL GUSTED / ETHEREAL SHE / RIDES
DAY—SHEERING:

(RIB CAGE)
IN THE FOG I HEAR MY NAME

THE HATE BRIGADE OF THE STATE &
NEIGHBORS / LOCALIZED REGIONALIZED
LEGITIMIZED BY EFFORT TOWARDS UN
-EVIDENCING GAVE LEGS TO THEIR FATAL
OCCUPATION / THUS THEY WALK / PARASITIC
EXPEDIENT / A TOOL OF THE CULLING

LIVID!
GHOSTS-SHE AIRS NIGHT—
NOT SEEKING PERMISSION
TO LIVE

AURAL CROWN SHEATHS
LOVING PARADE
SPECTRAL AUDIENCE AS LOVER OR
ANTAGONIST

EVERYONE LOVES THE WOMAN ON
STAGE
SHE IS WEARING THOSE JEANS
THAT GOWN
TORN

    HALLOW S END / TRAGIC STAR /
    SHRED GRACE

STRATEGIC PAUSE—
EVE,   BELTING:

    RODE 'ROUND MY RIDIN' 'ROUND
    / NOT HAVING IT— /
    IT S ALL SHOW / 4TH WALL A HOUSE MAKES

    NO VOTES IN THE THEATRE OF
    APOCALYPSE NO ENCORE FROM
    THE SPECTRE OF BURDEN

GRATE GRILL TO LIP COILED
THE CABLE JUST SO IN CAREFUL
ROUND PASSING VOICE HANDHELD

FROM LEFT›RIGHT LEFT ON
THE STOOL MACROPHONIC
SCREECHING TO MONITOR

(RIB CAGE)
IN THE FOG I HEAR MY NAME
—FUCK UP OUT MY WAY
RIDER RUNS ASTRAY (RIB CAGE)

on principle

I made an enemy of me, an enemy of me, I made—
an enemy of me, an enemy, of me I made an enemy. of me, I made
an enemy. of me, an enemy I made. an enemy of me, I made, an
enemy of me. I made an enemy of me, an enemy of me, I made an
enemy of me: an enemy. of me I made an enemy of me—

—I made an enemy of me
an enemy of me I made
an enemy of me
I made
an enemy
of me I made
an enemy

of me
I made   an enemy I made
an enemy I made
an enemy of me I made
an enemy of me an enemy I made
an enemy of me,

Heist Divination

ace in uneven water closes
distance of cornering four.

debt to undo,
ghost in the cup. risky dice, throw
your stakes. hell-bent on the heist—

I ve got nothing
to lose

(high are hopes of the chance habit.
[heist divination]. rest for the bet
on /rise. hope,   my bad habit,
praytowhomyoupray

game is demand, mingle power
& pattern, *mystic.*| || bonethrower,
ask not, to which she says
offer your measure

praise the weighted hand
delight & swift. there s a
chance that his luck may
change. gambles to shift
a steadfast heart.

to
chase a memory of the
kinds of talking we once
did w/ gods of our nature,
undead in the continuum
of inseparability. winning

could not be anything greater than that.   all
the game that I ve got, I give. play like I haven t noticed the street lights
cut on,   moths racing toward the warming bulb,   betting
everything on five minutes more. everything. to life   it all was
game.   no way I m coming up short.

so then play—
delight in listening pictures, torching cerasee, humbly chanting,
may they fall, like leaves may they fall
blow a wish in favor, (hand) cast no void

hunger

remakes
unfolds
creates
controls
undoes
devolves
sustains
prepares
involves
dissolves

me

//for some chiral obscenity, her
  talus-cast
  feeds the
lot of thieves.
odd guzzling eye digits
pattern s shifting
pulse//

ASK NOT // /
OFFER YOUR MEASURE

fickle-angled prayer
positions a favored vertex—)
act accordingly.

call me knuckle history. goat knuckle tails time. fate is a game—luck to who it draws. draws the luck of a trickster to be. draws a straw to her cubing. cube of all that s told. bonethrower, divine your needed now, your loaded vault. Read out its etch onto our haul—|| |

| || [throw

throw]

\\

_ stone bridges
_ velvet irises
_ iron tears
_ salted lots
_ eyes of the devil
_ demon sprouts
_ dirt analyses
_ rising suns
_ peerless angles
_ cups of blood
_ spindles of seaweed
_ undug moats
_ enamel spoons

_ glass die
_ knock-kneed horses
_ flaming needles
_ silver carts
_ leather baronettes
_ foamed honeydew
_ fissured roses
_ swinging swords, held by a hair
_ coot s nests
_ clapperless bells
_ fire-drowned stars
_ linen notebooks
_ seas of grasses
_ vulgar shuffles
_ feels of May
_ calcified orbs
_ moss lamb

|| |

(blows blessed cool on the weight in my cup, faceless until they call. colliding sand in my palm make clack, shake & relinquish. soft fist holding the noise of my lucky, heavy on the fall. shell held slime manifest. scatter a variable in cacophony. {number, I make do/I make due.} haul on out loot, bonethrower cast your highest—

last Thursday

for Gabrielle Octavia Rucker

over drinks at the bar above the theatre at the end of all that was familiar yesterday, she questions the fallings of little kings, nudging the black leather piece into its lanky isosceles slot, safe w/ its own for now. communal forms don t negate the need for, nor the sacredness of Secrecy. a long game, for real. you get out what you put in, & the rest is chance it seems.

what is left? what has not yet been done? we make our earthly return w/ cosmic determination, feudal resistance. we operate under honest direction, an earnest scarcity: live the short life w/ your hearth on your sleeve, ear to the ground. further still, she anticipated the chaos! apparently they all did, some even knew as children. I break into hive & tremor, as my spine remembers the frigid Pacific & how no one believed me.

of course it is devastating, & I won t hold back in telling you how: when it s raining out, & again power begets power. the state is unabashedly delighted in its carnage. yes, the year spent unable to beg, plead. eye of ice, heart of stone. yes, you ought to take it personally—growing pains well into old age.

her frustration becomes me, I carry it w/ me even now. *why are we back here?* we remain in a ponder, letting resentment sharpen around us as the porcupine teaches: *my body is my defense in the face of imminent enclosure, its talents remain unburied.*

sonorous in bitter utterances, performative dillydally: perhaps we re back to take a bow, detail the determining factors. this weather in which blood bursts from my fingers, sludges in my toes. cruel moon hangs high. & the dice again rolls.

SCRAM !

a heat pools to the center—
growl fed a wave
knaves,
fell in line

totally obsolete
ready to risk it all
totally understand

Perpetual,
Perpetual

shake   rattle   float   ultra|atrial

---

gratitude gyal

shadowy way—his grace faces north. the whistling arrows fail to make
pierce. marble curtain drapes the amphora. stomp, centaur, merciless
ground, restless for the buried skull. making two of it. find me, too.
leaves fall like footsteps on hickory knoll.
we boast the dawn of a new day.
the assassins could not reach me.

sweet (9/6)

            callaloo kisses, the
dumplings palm-rolled,
starfruit fresh picked.
bacalao, my baby.

we make a weird Caribbean—she affirms.

look: ackee red, orange, yellow, black.
sweet: gator pear butter soft.

mango seed sucked clean. what hair remains combed like an ugli fruit doll. soursop, sugarcane, gungo. we made home how we could. yesterday was four years long.

I grew greedy   *blasé, ain t you, daddy?*
two machetes left in the swindling.

my   june plum, sweet: your hand in mine. it rained daily
w/o you it rained.

birdwatcher polder-side, don t you know you saved my life?
you made me the girl of my dreams—

slither

my darling rolls pencil thin
I fawn at her every word

he leads w/ a little pinch
I bend w/ ambitious curve

for now there s impeding swell
she s drenched in a royal tulle

they excess the holy bell
I inhale her perfect pull

the oil of my fingers sear
onto the skin of this book

I sip at his perfect tear
he gives me that haunted look

w/ steadfast & knowing grace
I dare you to meet my eyes

I brush my hair from my nape
my darling, to my surprise ~

the pen s in the other hand
the canvas is acres thick

he writes faster than I can
cause that oughta do the trick

they re reading like scholarship
she undoes the rhythmic swirl

so pensive the effort spills
I m dying to be your girl

my darling rolls pencil thin
I fawn at her every word

I m losing a little bit
I bend w/ ambitious curve

[*it s allowed not allowed*
it s allowed   not allowed
it s not allowed
al   -lowed
it s allowed   all loud
it s not-so loud—
not so loud   all so loud it s allowed]

unruly temporalities unruly narrator, I m just looking to feel small in the right contexts—in the vast beauty of things preferably—for all I know is wildness. wilderness.   finds me when I m not looking, beckons when I call. takes over at night, howls til high noon.   into madness an alias by any other name,   alembic antagonist auspice antinomy afroandrogyny, we reek of it in good company. everybody here in it: squealing barometer kettleblack block w/ misery-midnight knowledges, darkness, smog & flash.   an earthen rumble inside the ravenous hive, the gospel of love & protest, let me go off for a minute.   the sounds of a world at its beginning, at its onto. transformation by any means.

get in there.
stay in it.

narrative at the level of the line, move the air as it demands.   greeting feedback grating amaranth permeating frankincense sliverlinger   smoke in the monolith,   the bones of the song begin shaking. latch on into grumbling welcome,   soundbitten bothering bother body gather liftpull, tear, pull, push-roll.   organic choreography, meanspirited when I need to be,   for the best of us.   queerseraphim black wing the night   vertiginous in the hardglowflickerfuckshutterblast blinking in the blistering sun, stunned out of ennui.   how lightning breeds thunder.   lightstems   that summon the long ago. glances gazes gauzes goozing shattered glass underfoot. what brings me to you is by definition rebellion together.   our breathing scream, a/symmetric sonics   breathes back life into what breathes for us,   bleeds us for. nihilist longevity, all praise   Daughters of Resentment, our soured tongues thirst for water, & we will not stop seeking our satisfaction until

we are unthirsty: that would be out of character! mouthfaint aroma, link
up in that outer, noisy   interiority. there is nothing & even there is
   life. eyes on you & in you, hold & heed. onto inner oculus. into ornate
orbitals, arbitrary. nonetheless,   nocturnal   masses.
notw/standing now I know what I know.

remedies III & IV (corpse pose)

in the eclipse, it is *fine for now.* just beyond the
bridge, but still at a center. snowshelf before
avalanche, electric cloud from above on &
off again, cruising potent quiet. spacious, yet
collective, cirrocumulus. *andante,*   vapor
undoes its conceal, condensing over eyelashes,
emboss surface everwet. how we learned to live
under frigid conditions. Fog   who consumes
the mouth of the Sun
                                        w/ the patience of a ballad—
bounding over this new morning, long before
morning & at day s end yet to burn off,
folding itself into night

                                        chrysalis. what made it bearable
—lovely, even—was how efforted, one step solid
in any direction, elbows akinder. feet on ground,
longstanding ceremony, acutely aware in our
perfect flailing space. call me up out slumber—
transition, too,
is a state. you by my side of your own volition.
humbling to me, humming to me. leads me
sweetly to lakesedge, her dipping braid in hand,
exhibiting other densities. at its end, ascertain
we exit new, committed to fragrant possibility:
at an arm s length,
across an ocean, should it be that way for a while.

we were compelled

after/towards Greg Tate & Burnt Sugar the Arkestra Chamber, after/towards the band(s)

a brightness pulled us forth. we were drawn into this formation.
impulse charged in copper vein. familiars made hammers of
nimble fingers. to the thrill of a nonstandard, silver makes
chill of aquarian directive, an acoustic transparency. wilted
cartography on the podium, baritone in nature. we relay an
evermoving text, our assignment, search, & commitment.
turning to face you now,
I catch your anxious sigh,
short & pushed tightly.
the stakes were that we might fail to hear one another, or that
we would not move on from this place. nonetheless, we were
compelled. lamentations climb from coccyx, tail led: standing
music, sitting music. attendance made apparent we had already
begun. attendance made obvious the risk of audience. it could
not be resolved. what could we make if we fear the material?
matter amassing forge ecstatic. we refute the consumptive
encounter in any variation, passive or captive. if you cannot
comply, you are welcome to leave. our compulsion is built on
vast coinciding acts of *this is*
what
I
have to give—take it   freely.
at last—you look up, swamp-eyed. *we will go far*
from here, you make promise. *I am all out of rehearsals*, you
declare. *it was too late to turn our back to the real thing, our real*

lives. we have already waited far long.—yes, we were compelled.
conductor, let fall the baton. I m your associate. what we lift
wrestled back in our hands: trout wrestling forth fight, scales
slicing sore at prying greed (I could not let go—I could not
say why: committed to a tradition I seek to become old in,
I know it all too simply. I aspire to the privilege of becoming
old, sustaining an eagerness to be an active & willing
participant in a thriving exaltation. what I
want for us all), until then its gasp slows. it bounds back
forward into a heaving water, enunciating perfect splash
—we, in turn, gasp. what we made wrestled back in our
hands, suntouched arrivant s karmic palmetto. arcana
shuffle heralds buoyant.
for it to be consistent,
it had to be dangerous. living instrument, encourage your
utter. our voice coil curls in sensation. precious tremble
floods nerve. band, our listening unit & politic, actress of
sound, we witness as one our resulting urgencies, witness
to those who witness the sound.

proceed, swamp-eyed.
take as long as you need.
I m your audience right now
—my play is my applause.
love made work of our hands.

sloe string

her rosewood hollowbody stains the imagination—w/ her, the glamour of good wood cut unique. she plays a creaking house rotational, pressing it to her body. the centennial stairway cracked & strung together moans accordion. nation is a problem she plays in her hands. stringing the drumhead s hull, armed to refute. this technology surrounds like a bad mood. folk, this plan—ever-updated—passed on, beat down a pitter-patter, strung up the snare, screeching up the bow. voices in negotiation. as is. now slick fingers to make the people dance—or what? Juke-Universe. Boo rasps hot a souped-up blue, tryna make sense of sloe. waiting outside, she s chattin' by way of the guitar—as to manifest manos the ego, strummed apart bloodied. hand arpeggios voice, finger-picking the mourning of the erred, groaning slushy. hammering on about this harmonic; even silence knows your anonym.

together we sit in a general conversation, now then let it be conversational. convexing this unyielding pursuit of rotary comprehension. watching from the balcony, the stage houses a cinema: light fog, house up fifty, maybe sixty. the gathered refused dark begs your full participation, the ensemble cast from the assembled. from the hole whines a voice, wails up fortune s sorrow—an encompassed feel I am enthralled to feel. there would be days like this. scratching it out longhand, all up the neck, worn in the groove. slick this broom all cross the floor, dust ash out to storm. longhand all out to sea. clear my mind for a little while, let my hair do the talking. strum rotary a spinning purr coiled steel strings out the skull. these strings tether me to the world. I play them for you. resonant bending metal, the silent field of magnetics reveals elliptical manifest, echo chamber refutes the original. bending 6 twist out her puncture, a chunk that throws—in the booth screamin' *give 'em more hair.* heavy foot floats **overd**rive pushed to clip. a strained serenity makes squeal of the tube—that s why they call it the champ! still in pursuit of that chime—

stereo/field

angel s ostinato composition storm composite / loop to root incomplete / reel-born / informula / amplify riff / empty out all day / all sudden sludge / p o w e r chord rearing thought s voice / gouging w h o le / grin false in capillary structure / stance s t i ll pump / artery root s rib / heart s rib raw / p o w e r chor d s softshock / steel to doom rapturous / dome acquiesce / subtle teeth / the city we are is our undoing

if there can only be decorative ideas then say so—
wield tongue in fist, held sharpened to ruin—

a rising gift of tenor,   accessible w/ eunuch ease

— let it then rise

500 Fingers of Drill~

did you not hear her? *ambient is over*

— let it then rise

this heirless throne s   empty almanac
dry architexture   veneer fad
disco averno   gritted teeth grate to dust
grim s arid shrine remains to be seen

\\ damning inculcation \\
\\ faith in erasure \\
\\ golden shadow make sick-splayed nation \\ the clutch
of shadow
pumps false

woman nodes the world Anthems. Atlas.
nth at a split fulls the herd s
quartzing crush—

whipped sloppy   /hop in
adored in hormonic wealth
salvation s purging window   rummaging heaven s sphincter

damning incantation
faith in peculiar
there   under there

pace is the cage

“

hollow roam due west, a pulse that
ponders floats.   stage paces an antagonism.
have at it mutable world | mutable word your worst—

target audience: eyes trained on the revolution. rise, you
ruinous jury shaped for a justing to
be seen, lined for the precursive event

certified headbanger—rubbernecked knocker
been trouble   been been
rid

of me
mischief fits   you   nicely
mischief amplifies bodyinggroan   full stack

,   righteous collapse we make
of terrible ordained. together
we mold this delicate thing.

go sledge to my swing
go   sledge to my   swing
go swung to my   ledger

hood upheaval—wisdom s tactile
grandeur in the   measure of
ancestor & heiress are you,   intuition.

seek your   knowing
dark   for it to be ours
it has to be yours—an impossible   sustain

sustains us
   stains us
          Sustanzas

: disobedient remedies
                                                    a hopeful
few remain— the revolution slipped

their ropes. so deep their love for us.
inclined to   our mis
-behavior—let the real in

we aid your falling light—
emergent flame.
sweet|sweat, movement   "

accommodates shift. futile we aid
                          flame—it comes from
the chest. undercarry weaving

smear   gaining let-
go bygetting out the way
oral drift dissolves a throating strained

face us in epileptic dark | cage effervesces
raze to wringing step | concentric tantrum
march | limbing toss | wailing pontification:

double down in anticipation of blowout—
what we hear is the wait
circle up *set me up for a good time*

ddoubled-down in anticipation of blow-up
what we hear is the wait
stir the earth, the heated air bellows

hot in the volume anticipatory
gratitude in wait of this hallowed
stir the air, the heated earth belches

forth humming perimeter, full stack
grazing elevation s sweetgrass —if
I jump from here I ll fly

notes&acknowledgments

Love is Earth's mission
despite the massed dead.
—Anthony McNeill, *Chinese Lanterns from the Blue Child*

In the premises of the tongue
dwells the anarchy of the ear ;
in the chaos of the vision
resolution of the purpose.
—Martin Carter, *Poems of Succession*

These poems have been embodied & inscribed between the fall of Grenfell Tower; the onset & ongoing weaponized mismanagement of the COVID-19 pandemic; the rampant genocides taking place in Congo, Palestine, Sudan, Haiti, & elsewhere; the global surge of nationalist attitudes & anti-immigration movements; a steady uptick of legislation & rhetoric unabashedly encouraging violence towards trans & queer peoples, especially youth; the ancestoring of Kamau Brathwaite, Rana Zoe Mungin, Keona Veronica Kettle, Roberta Flack, Nikki Giovanni, bell hooks, Tahjay Dobson/TDott Woo, Greg Tate, Kelli Hand/K-Hand, April Freely, Perla Zuñiga, William Pope.L, Gboyega Odubanjo, Dr. Refaat Alareer, Benjamin Zephaniah, Lorraine O'Grady, Assata Shakur, Miss Major, & D'Angelo—if only to name a few of those who by their word & breath have shown me a way that life can be conducted—& the accelerating catastrophes resulting from climate crisis. The price for opposing fascism is censorship most moderately, voice/breath/life most critically. I do not neglect what new life & survival efforts persist despite these thefts & violences, but it would be amiss not to name these anchoring injustices & heartbreaks, the purview we endure & imagine against. I am not jaded, or forcefully cheerful about our days—nor am I numb to the casualness of casualty. Love: no small, nor singular thing. I live in Earth's mission—& too, I mourn the amassed. I listen for their song—

o

"remedies I" was previously included in r. erica doyle's Academy of American Poets' Poem-a-Day curation in 2021. An earlier version of "remedies V" was commissioned by Taylor Johnson during his 2022 Guggenheim Poetry Fellowship. "remedies II" was published in Elderly 33 & 1/3, guest edited by Angel Dominguez. "us girls" was previously published on Poem-a-Day in 2023, guest edited by Eunsong Kim. "last Thursday" was published in *The Recluse*. "to a well another, , , ," was written in response to Jordi de Vetten's photobook of the same title; the poem appears as the cover of the book. "IN COMMON KIND // BODYFAST" collects the titles of my photographic works included in "BODY LANGUAGE", curated by David Lindsay & exhibited at the Poetry Project in 2024. "a/mercurial" was previously published in *What Tells You Ripeness: Black Poets on Nature*, published by Pangyrus & guest edited by Nikki Wallschlaeger. An earlier version of "Never created, never destroyed" exists as a short film made in collaboration w/ Ryan C. Clarke, & includes animations by RaFia Santana. The text of that versioning was also published in 1080PRESS' newsletter series. The poem cites Scott MacDonald's interview w/ David Greaves, published in *William Greaves: Filmmaking as Mission*, edited by MacDonald & Jacqueline Najuma Stewart. "unruly temporalities" is vocalized on Dreamcrusher's *Another Country*, 2020. "in & for voices" interpolates Fela Kuti's "Coffin for Head of State" (surely no ceremony for the fall of our oppressors). David Hammons' sculpture, "Bird", his tribute to Charlie Parker, appears in the mind's eye of "ghetto sonetto foul play (exist strategy) *grave*". "sundew" references Amina Claudine Myers' instruments played on *Songs for Mother E*, 1980. "borrowed image" references the first track of Miles Davis' 1974 album, *Get Up with It*. "PRACTICE *ETERNAL*" quotes Galaxy 2 Galaxy's "Transition", from *A Hitech Jazz Compilation*, 2005. "sweet (9/6)" quotes "Blasé", the second track of Archie Shepp's 1969 album of the same title, penned & vocalized by Jeanne Lee. "remedies III & IV (corpse pose)" references the second track of Unwound's 1996 album, *Repetition*. "ambient is over" is quoted from a tweet by L'Rain. "stereo/field" meditates & diverges onward from Janiva Ellis' *StackedPlot*, presented at 47 Canal. My thanks to the editors, publishers, & laborers that make these publications possible.

o

Some of these poems &/or their cadences found their shape in sonic collaborations & improvised performances w/ an overlapping & far-reaching cohort of mischief. We rehearse a diaspora; may it spill further over: senakirfa A., Viana Afoumou, Justin Allen, Hannah Black, Soraya Lutangu Bonaventure, Sol Cabrini, Taja Cheek, Ryan C. Clarke, Dreamcrusher, Dweller Electronics, Ladipo Famodu, Yulan Grant, Yohannes Henriksson, Alec Mateo, Charleen McClure, Nicole Miller, Shala Miller, mhm, mhm, M.L. Thomas, Tavish Timothy, Phantom Wizard, & Geo Wyex. Thank you for your invitations & for receiving mine. Evermore my gratitude floods.

Further flooding gratitude for their support, conversation, co-study, teachings: Chanelle Adams, Amal Alhaag, Bea Ortega Botas, Maxe Crandall, LaTasha N. Nevada Diggs, Shakira Evans, Moa Holgersson, Joselia Rebekah Hughes, Imani Elizabeth Jackson, dove/Christine Kirubi, Jasmine Lee, Yaniya Lee,

Nabi Lovelace, Daniel Neumann, Emma Olson, Oluremi C. Onabanjo, Danny Sadiel Peña, M. NourbeSe Philip, Gabrielle Octavia Rucker, Nell Schwan, Jayson P. Smith, Jay Tan, Xiomara Virdó, Leto Ybarra, & Constantina Zavistanos. My love & thanks to senakirfa, Joey de Jesus, Sumia Juxun, & Geo for their committed & close reading of *PACES THE CAGE* as it moulted. We are altogether less alone in haptic language.

Ben Estes & Alan Felsenthal: as editors & publishers, you lead w/ your hearts—a gift to be held in such care & attention. Thank you for your dedication to letting this book grow into what it wanted to be.

Derica Shields—lawlessly yours—thrumming wings to soar.

OTHER TITLES FROM THE SONG CAVE:

1. *A Dark Dreambox of Another Kind* by **Alfred Starr Hamilton**
2. *My Enemies* by **Jane Gregory**
3. *Rude Woods* by **Nate Klug**
4. *Georges Braque and Others* by **Trevor Winkfield**
5. *The Living Method* by **Sara Nicholson**
6. *Splash State* by **Todd Colby**
7. *Essay Stanzas* by **Thomas Meyer**
8. *Illustrated Games of Patience* by **Ben Estes**
9. *Dark Green* by **Emily Hunt**
10. *Honest James* by **Christian Schlegel**
11. *M* by **Hannah Brooks-Motl**
12. *What the Lyric Is* by **Sara Nicholson**
13. *The Hermit* by **Lucy Ives**
14. *The Orchid Stories* by **Kenward Elmslie**
15. *Do Not Be a Gentleman When You Say Goodnight* by **Mitch Sisskind**
16. *HAIRDO* by **Rachel B. Glaser**
17. *Motor Maids across the Continent* by **Ron Padgett**
18. *Songs for Schizoid Siblings* by **Lionel Ziprin**
19. *Professionals of Hope: The Selected Writings of* **Subcomandante Marcos**
20. *Fort Not* by **Emily Skillings**
21. *Riddles, Etc.* by **Geoffrey Hilsabeck**
22. *CHARAS: The Improbable Dome Builders* by **Syeus Mottel**
    (Co-published with Pioneer Works)
23. *YEAH NO* by **Jane Gregory**

24. *Nioque of the Early-Spring* by **Francis Ponge**

25. *Smudgy and Lossy* by **John Myers**

26. *The Desert* by **Brandon Shimoda**

27. *Scardanelli* by **Friederike Mayröcker**

28. *The Alley of Fireflies and Other Stories* by **Raymond Roussel**

29. *CHANGES: Notes on Choreography* by **Merce Cunningham** (Co-published with the Merce Cunningham Trust)

30. *My Mother Laughs* by **Chantal Akerman**

31. *Earth* by **Hannah Brooks-Motl**

32. *Everything and Other Poems* by **Charles North**

33. *Paper Bells* by **Phan Nhiên Hạo**

34. *Photographs: Together & Alone* by **Karlheinz Weinberger**

35. *A Better Place Is Hard to Find* by **Aaron Fagan**

36. *Rough Song* by **Blanca Varela**

37. *In the Same Light: 200 Poems for Our Century From the Migrants & Exiles of the Tang Dynasty,* translated by **Wong May**

38. *On the Mesa: An Anthology of Bolinas Writing (50th Anniversary Edition),* edited by **Ben Estes and Joel Weishaus**

39. *Listen My Friend, This Is the Dream I Dreamed Last Night* by **Cody-Rose Clevidence**

40. *Poetries* by **Georges Schehadé**

41. *Wings in Time* by **Callie Garnett**

42. *Two Murals* by **Jesús Castillo**

43. *Punks: New & Selected Poems* by **John Keene**

44. *ABC Moonlight* by **Ben Estes**

45. *Star Lake* by **Arda Collins**

46. *The Maybe-Bird* by **Jennifer Elise Foerster**

47. *Seriously Well* by **Helge Torvund**

48. *Dereliction* by **Gabrielle Octavia Rucker**

49. *Bookworm: Conversations with* **Michael Silverblatt**

50. *April* by **Sara Nicholson**

51. *Valley of the Many-Colored Grasses* by **Ronald Johnson**

52. *The Sphinx and the Milky Way: Selections from the Notebooks of* **Charles Burchfield**

53. *Telling the Truth as It Comes Up: Selected Talks & Essays 1991–2018* by **Alice Notley**

54. *Lunar Solo: Selected Poems* by **Jules Laforgue**

55. *Stranger* by **Emily Hunt**

56. *The Selkie* by **Morgan Võ**

57. *Hereafter* by **Alan Felsenthal**

58. *Cold Dogs* by **Zan de Parry**

59. *Saturday* by **Margaret Ross**

60. *Many Poems* by **Roberta Iannamico**

61. *Ultraviolet of the Genuine* by **Hannah Brooks-Motl**

62. *Silkworm's Pansori* by **David Seung**

63. *Tantrums in Air* by **Emily Skillings**

64. *Jump Cuts: Essays on Surrealism, Film, Music, Culture, and Other Utopian Topics* by **Mark Polizzotti**

65. *Earthly: Selected Poems* by **Jean Follain**

66. *Nebraska* by **George Whitmore**

67. *Behind the State Capitol: Or Cincinnati Pike* by **John Wieners**